UNTOLD STORIES OF AFRICA

AFRICA AT ITS PRIDE

BY

LINDA LONG

TABLE OF CONTENT

INTRODUCTION

I've been perusing the content for a film about Sara Forbes Bonetta. In the event that the name is new, she carried on with a surprising nineteenth century English life and a film ought to be made about her.

She was naturally introduced to Yoruba eminence north-east of Lagos in 1843, and named Aina. Yet, after five years, her town was assaulted by those notorious female Amazons of Dahomey (the present Benin Republic). Her folks were killed in the assault and she got herself both a vagrant and a slave.

All the more emphatically still, she was saved by her capturer, Ruler Ghezo, to be customarily forfeited, just for a meeting English designation under one Skipper Forbes to supplication for her to be saved (obviously cash changed hands). Aina was renamed by Forbes, with the boat she cruised on to Britain - the HMS Bonetta - his motivation for her last name. In London, she was acquainted with Sovereign Victoria, who fancied the bright little kid (she'd learnt English and French on the journey) and took her on as her goddaughter.

That a thoughtful individual of color was an affectionate piece of the English illustrious court has basically a passing relegraciousvance today, considering that Ruler Harry's better half, Meghan Markle, is biracial - part white European and part African-American.

In the event that a regal wedding continues, will the court of Windsor be pretty much as inviting as a long time back, or, given an entertainer may be Sara Forbes Bonetta, naturally introduced to Yoruba sovereignty approach Lagos in 1843, was taken on as a goddaughter by Sovereign thought about one bar under an everyday person, could a demeanor of froideur win?

Be that as it may, there is a more profound idea: the content prompts past the foam of a superstar possibly wedding into nobility. It is that such countless phenomenal African lives and circumstances remain unnarrated and undocumented, and the sheer variety of African experience goes through the tightest channel into portrayal, quiet and shared mindset.

As per a 2013 Harvard study, the main 20 most different countries on the planet are all in Africa (with Uganda being the most ethnically different country on earth), though Europe is the least ethnically different landmass in the world.

There is in this way a reverse connection between territorial variety and the "content" - books, films and different media - that is delivered. While there are vast movies about Western experience - WWII being a urgent storyline (with more than 1,300 movies about this occasion alone) - there are insufficient few movies about wars - to keep to a similar subject - that occurred on the African mainland, with a significant number of the most popular Hollywood movies (Zulu, Blood Precious stone, and Ruler of Battle to pick a speedy three) typically zeroing in on white heroes.

Right now, in any event some of you will think: what might be said about Nollywood? The Nigerian famous entertainment world produces film by the cart load, doubtlessly it is a significant restorative?

The response is no. The Nigerian entertainment world, basically at this stage in its turn of events, does scarcely anything to offset white outlining of the story. Despite the fact that creation values have improved, the storylines are as yet two dimensional, with little interest in authentic movies (for certain prominent exemptions, for example, '76), or to be sure characters like Sara Forbes Bonetta.

Ostensibly, Nollywood has been separating into two in the past couple of years: into films which duplicate dark American film (rom coms) or keep on slandering conventional social qualities with changing levels of nuance.

On the scholarly front, in spite of the rising interest in African composition, the outer layer of the mainland's plenty of stories still can't seem to really be damaged. It is empowering that distributors like Cassava Republic, Parresia and Kachifo in Nigeria, as well as Kwani? Also, Storymoja in Kenya and others somewhere else have been making waves of interest in new kinds of African composition, breaking assumptions and going a long way past the social patriotism of a very long time ago. Be that as it may, these are little organizations making a stream of stories (with practically no linkages to the entertainment world or the diversion area at large) compared to the powerful waterways moving from the substance creation focuses of London and New York.

The impact of these two Western capitals of account creation slants African stories for socalled worker fiction - the diasporic experience as retold by Chimamanda Adichie, Imbolo Mbue or Tope Folarin.

There is an immense hole with respect to characters and places untold. From my time in Nigeria, I long for anecdotes about the "Nok individuals" who made the unimaginable earthenware heads quite a while back, or for nonexistent investigations of individuals that made the really old and baffling Ikom stone monuments in the south-east. Or on the other hand, moving concentration, a film about the most extravagant man ever, Mansa Musa I and his legendary journey to Mecca in 1324.

While Amin Maalouf composed an impressive record of Leo Africanus and his journey around north Africa in the sixteenth hundred years, the element film still can't seem to be made (albeit Mauritanian auteur Abderrahmane Sissako has essentially thought to be the venture).

Yet, even these thoughts are simple, pushing a finger profound past the surface. What might be said about an African adaptation of Pharaonic Kemet (impacted by Cheikh Anta Diop) as a cure to Ridley Scott's tragically white Departure: Divine beings and Rulers? Or on the other hand, wandering south, a clever that brings alive the Realm of Kush (and their pyramids at Meroe), or, toward the west, the strong Kanem-Bornu domain (which rose in 700 AD and endured almost seven centuries), or a lot further south, stories from the hour of Extraordinary Zimbabwe. Or on the other hand what might be said about additional movies about the conflict that Nigeria seethed on itself - A big part of a

Yellow Sun is unquestionably sufficiently not.

Whole realms lie quiet, covered under sand and earth, not a single film group to be seen. Legends and courageous women, bad guys and adversaries stay pageless. On one level, this is basically a shortfall of creative mind and a lost business opportunity.

The furious progress of Nollywood across the mainland has been essentially determined by acknowledgment: seeing oneself (or comparable forms of oneself) reflected has an intrinsic worth, particularly as an offset to the predominantly white portrayals and inclination given forward from Hollywood.

The gigantic ongoing rat outcome of The Wedding Party in Nigeria - with film industry returns of N200m ($630,000) in only 16 days - pushes future prospects.

What amount more effective could well
known African film be, assuming that it
began to take advantage of a portion of the
genuinely incredible stories that uncovered
an African past just as self important and
nuanced as Europe's?

In any case, once more, on a far more
profound level, taking advantage of the
mainland's immense document of untold
stories isn't just about income. It is about an
aggregate clairvoyant rebalancing, away from
a primarily white Judeo-Christian semiotics
and a feeling of ceaseless subliminal social
relocation, towards an African arrangement
of story paradigms and pathways into what's
to come.

The Yoruba divine beings alone can equal the
Antiquated Greeks for nuance, show and
interest. There is doubtlessly an elusive yet

strong wellbeing in this turn, making a feeling of the longue durée - a continuum of energy and imagination that approves the spirits and predeterminations of a billion Africans.

As both America and Europe turn in on themselves, towards political and monetary protectionism and discontinuity and being decreased to the unadulterated amount of their parts in the years ahead, there will definitely be ramifications for Africa. Social protectionism will probably continue in the wake, and the mainland might be left alone on all fronts. The post-oil future that entices is an indication that African items will be less vital for the worldwide economy. Africa won't be commended for rising, or sympathized with for falling, it will just be passed on to its own destiny.

This is a radiant chance for an inside discussion to start with the assumption that there are however many stories as there is dark gold, across all quadrants of the landmass.

In spite of winning hypotheses, it is maybe not wares, nor ability, nor organizations nor even advancement that animates improvement. Rather, it is when individuals all in all can gather the best assets from the past to conjure up another future that the wizardry of aggregate social cognizance can get going

A more engaged predetermination starts as a matter of some importance with recovering and reexamining stories that ground the aggregate self in forerunners and indeed, grandness.

Which takes me back to Sara Forbes Bonetta.
Tragically, the Sovereign's extraordinary
goddaughter never accomplished full
wellbeing in wet Dickensian England. She
passed on from TB and matured at only 37.
Her body lies in a plain grave in a burial
ground in Funchal, Madeira. Her story still
needs to be told.

HISTORICAL BACKDROP

The historical backdrop of current people started in Africa. Then, at that point, it is nothing unexpected that Africa was once home to a few incredible old developments. A portion of these civilizations existed over centuries prior, while others prospered all the more as of late. These civilizations frequently assembled incredible designs that were wonders of the old world. Generally speaking, these designs actually stand today. Generally, the flourishing of Africa's old human advancements was profoundly subject to exchange and the trading of information. Eventually, the landmass' all old civic establishments met their end, however not prior to leaving an enduring inheritance on individuals they once dominated. The following are eight of Africa's most prominent old civic establishments.

Antiquated Egypt is seemingly the most notable of Africa's old developments. It started around 3400 BCE. Initially, there were two Egyptian realms. One was Upper Egypt, which was situated in what is currently focal and southern Egypt, along the Nile Waterway. The other realm was Lower Egypt, based principally in the Nile Delta district of present-day northern Egypt. In 3100 BCE, Ruler Menes of Upper Egypt vanquished Lower Egypt and joined the two realms. During the time of the Old Realm (c. 2686 - 2181 BCE), the Egyptians fabricated the pyramids for which the antiquated progress is most popular, including the Incomparable Pyramid, which is one of the Seven Miracles of the Old World.

The Realm of Kush thrived between c. 1069 BCE and 350 CE. It controlled a huge wrap of an area along the Nile Waterway in what is presently northern Sudan. The realm was a monetary focus that worked a rewarding exchange of ivory, incense, iron, and gold. It was both an exchanging accomplice and opponent of old Egypt toward the north. As a matter of fact, in the eighth century BCE, the Kushites vanquished Egypt, laying out the 25th Egyptian Tradition, which would lead Egypt for over a long time. The region encompassing the antiquated Kushite capital of Meroe is currently home to the remnants of north of 200 pyramids - a greater number of pyramids than in all of Egypt.

There is no conclusive agreement on where antiquated Dropkick was found. In any case, most researchers accept it was arranged some place in East Africa, potentially along the Red Ocean coast as well as present-day northwestern Somalia, Djibouti, and Eritrea. The realm was laid out around the year 2500

BCE. The majority of what is presently realized about old Dropkick comes from antiquated Egyptian sources, which hold that the realm was wealthy in midnight, gold, myrrh, and fascinating creatures like gorillas and panthers. Egypt was a significant exchange accomplice of Dropkick. Dropkick likewise affected antiquated Egypt. Truth be told, the antiquated Egyptians accepted that Dropkick was their place of beginning, referring to it as "the Place that is known for the Divine beings."

Carthage started as a city-state in what is presently Tunisia around the eighth or ninth century BCE. The city was worked by Phoenician pioneers, who relocated to the area from old Lebanon. In the end, Carthage developed into a distant farming domain, which controlled enormous pieces of beach front North Africa, the southern Iberian

Promontory, and all or part of the Mediterranean islands of Corsica, Sardinia, and Sicily. At its level, Carthage itself had a populace of almost a portion of 1,000,000 occupants. By the mid-third century BCE, the Carthaginian Domain clashed with another old incredible power, the Roman Realm, which prompted the Punic Conflicts. These conflicts finished in 146 BCE.

The Realm of Aksum existed from about the fourth century BCE to the tenth century CE in what is currently Eritrea and Ethiopia. It is felt that the realm was the Scriptural Ark of the Contract's resting place and the country of the Sovereign of Sheba. By the second and third hundreds of years CE, Aksum was an exchanging goliath and fundamental channel for exchange between old Europe and the Far East. Its most significant wares were gold and ivory. Aksum was among the principal realms to embrace Christianity. By the seventh or eighth hundreds of years CE, the realm went into decline, however its strict heritage actually exists as the Ethiopian Standard Church.

The Mali Realm arose in the thirteenth century CE and went on until the sixteenth century CE. It generally owed its prosperity to the huge gold stores inside its area, which comprised an enormous wrap of West Africa, from the Atlantic Sea to the line between present-day Mali and Niger. As a matter of fact, at a certain point, the Mali Realm was remembered to have delivered 66% of the world's whole gold stock. The individual accepted to be the realm's most noteworthy ruler, Mansa Musa, who controlled during the mid fourteenth hundred years, was rich to the point that his abundance is unfathomable even by the present norms. Subject to the Mali Realm, the city of Timbuktu, presently situated in present-day Mali, turned into a conspicuous focus of learning in the Islamic world.

The Songhai Realm was shaped in the fifteenth hundred years. It incorporated a portion of the regions previously heavily influenced by the Mali Domain. Truth be told, the Songhai Domain to a great extent supplanted the Mali Realm as the unmistakable power in the locale. At its level, the Songhai Realm was greater than all of Western Europe. It owed its prosperity to vivacious exchange strategies and a modern regulatory arrangement of government. Like the Mali Domain, the Songhai Realm additionally controlled Timbuktu at one time, opening many Islamic schools in the city. The Songhai capital, Gao, had a population of 100,000.

Zimbabwe is the name of an old city situated in the present-day nation of Zimbabwe. As a matter of fact, the nation of Zimbabwe is named after the old city. Some of the time called Incredible Zimbabwe, the city was made out of forcing stone walls and different other stone designs. The name "Zimbabwe" in the language of the native Shona individuals signifies "stone houses." The city traces all the way back to the tenth 100 years, however, between the thirteenth and fifteenth hundreds of years, it was the focal point of a tremendous realm, which controlled a huge lump of an area in present-day Botswana, Zimbabwe, and Mozambique. The realm had an economy in light of dairy cattle farming, crop development, and the exchange of gold on the shoreline of the Indian Sea. Oddly enough, Extraordinary Zimbabwe was deserted in the fifteenth 100 years. At its level, it was home to an expected 20,000 individuals.

30 THINGS ABOUT AFRICA

1.Mankind is of African origin. The most seasoned known skeletal remaining parts of physically present day people (or homo sapiens) were unearthed at locales in East Africa. Human remaining parts were found at Omo in Ethiopia that were dated at 195,000 years of age, the most established known on the planet.

2. Skeletons of pre-people have been tracked down in Africa that date back somewhere in the range of 4 and 5 million years. The most seasoned known hereditary kind of mankind is remembered to have been the australopithecus ramidus, who inhabited at least 4.4 a long time back.

3. Africans were quick to arrange fishing trips quite a while back. At Katanda, a district in northeastern Zaïre (presently Congo), was recuperated from a finely created series of spear focuses, all extravagantly cleaned and spiked. Likewise revealed was an instrument, similarly very much created, accepted to be a blade. The disclosures proposed the presence of an early amphibian or fishing based culture.

4. Africans were quick to participate in mining quite a while back. In 1964 a hematite mine was found in Swaziland at Bomvu Edge in the Ngwenya mountain range. Eventually 300,000 ancient rarities were recuperated including a huge number of stone-made mining instruments. Adrian Boshier, one of the archeologists on the site, dated the mine to a stunning 43,200 years of age.

5. Africans spearheaded fundamental number-crunching a long time back. The Ishango bone is a device handle with scores cut into it found in the Ishango locale of Zaïre (presently called Congo) close to Lake Edward. The bone instrument was initially remembered to have been north of 8,000 years of age, however a more delicate ongoing dating has given dates of 25,000 years of age. On the device are 3 lines of indents. Column 1 shows three scores cut close to six, four cut close to eight, ten cut close to two fives lastly a seven. The 3 and 6, 4 and 8, and 10 and 5, address the most common way of multiplying. Column 2 shows eleven scores cut close to 21 indents, and nineteen indents cut close to nine indents. This addresses 10 + 1, 20 + 1, 20 - 1 and 10 - 1. At long last, Line 3 shows eleven indents, thirteen scores, seventeen indents and nineteen indents. 11, 13, 17 and 19 are

the indivisible numbers somewhere in the range of 10 and 20.

6. Africans developed crops quite a while back, the main known progress in farming. Teacher Fred Wendorf found that individuals in Egypt's Western Desert developed harvests of grain, escapades, chick-peas, dates, vegetables, lentils and wheat. Their antiquated apparatuses were likewise recuperated. There were grindstones, processing stones, cutting sharp edges, conceal scrubbers, etching bruins, and mortars and pestles.

7. Africans preserved their dead quite a while back. A preserved newborn child was found under the Uan Muhuggiag rock cover in south western Libya. The newborn child was covered in the fetal position and was preserved utilizing an extremely complex procedure that probably required many years

to develop. The method originates before the earliest mummies known in Old Egypt by somewhere around 1,000 years. Scientifically measuring is dubious however the mummy might date from 7438 (±220) BC.

8. Africans cut the world's most memorable monster form at least a long time back. The Incomparable Sphinx of Giza was molded with the top of a man joined with the body of a lion. A key and significant inquiry raised by this landmark was: How old is it? In October 1991 Teacher Robert Schoch, a geologist from Boston College, exhibited that the Sphinx was etched between 5000 BC and 7000 BC, dates that he thought about moderate.

9. On the 1 Walk 1979, the New York Times conveyed an article on its first page likewise page sixteen that was entitled Nubian Government called Most seasoned. In this

article we were guaranteed that: "Proof of the most established unmistakable government in mankind's set of experiences, going before the ascent of the earliest Egyptian rulers by a few ages, has been found in curios from old Nubia" (for example the domain of the northern Sudan and the southern part of current Egypt.)

10. The antiquated Egyptians had similar kind of hot and humidity adjusted skeletal extents as current Dark Africans. A 2003 paper showed up in American Diary of Actual Human sciences by Dr Sonia Zakrzewski entitled Variety in Old Egyptian Height and Body Extents where that's what she expresses: "The crude qualities in Table 6 propose that Egyptians had the 'super-Negroid' body plan depicted by Robins (1983). The qualities for the brachial and crural files show that the distal fragments of

every appendage are longer comparative with the proximal portions than in many 'African' populaces."

11. The old Egyptians had Afro brushes. One essayist lets us know that the Egyptians "fabricated an exceptionally striking scope of brushes in ivory: the state of these is unmistakably African and resembles the brushes utilized even today by Africans and those of African plunge."

12. The Funerary Complex in the antiquated Egyptian city of Saqqara is the most seasoned building that sightseers routinely visit today. An external wall, presently for the most part in ruins, encompassed the entire design. Through the entry are a progression of sections, the primary stone-fabricated segments known to students of history. The North House additionally has decorative sections incorporated into the walls that have

papyrus-like capitals. Likewise inside the complex is the Stylized Court, made of limestone obstructs that have been quarried and afterward formed. In the focal point of the complex is the Step Pyramid, the first of 90 Egyptian pyramids.

13. The main Extraordinary Pyramid of Giza, the most remarkable structure ever, was a stunning 481 feet tall - what might be compared to a 40-story building. It was made of 2.3 million blocks of limestone and rock, some weighing 100 tons.

14. The antiquated Egyptian city of Kahun was the world's previously arranged city. Rectangular and walled, the city was separated into two sections. One section housed the more well off occupants - the copyists, authorities and foremen. The other part housed the standard individuals. The roads of the western segment specifically,

were straight, spread out on a matrix, and crossed each other at right points. A stone drain, over a portion of a meter wide, ran down the focal point of each and every road.

15. Egyptian houses were found in Kahun - each flaunting 70 rooms, partitioned into four areas or quarters. There was an expert's quarter, quarters for ladies and workers, quarters for workplaces lastly, quarters for storehouses, each confronting a focal patio. The expert's quarters had an open court with a stone water tank for washing. Encompassing this was a corridor.

16 The Maze in the Egyptian city of Hawara with its huge design, various yards, chambers and corridors, was the exceptionally biggest structure in ancient times. Flaunting 3,000 rooms, 1,500 of them were over the ground and the other 1,500 were underground.

17. Latrines and sewerage frameworks existed in antiquated Egypt. One of the pharaohs constructed a city presently known as Amarna. That's what an American metropolitan organizer noticed: "Extraordinary significance was connected to tidiness in Amarna as in other Egyptian urban areas. Latrines and sewers were being used to arrange squander. Cleanser was made for washing the body. Aromas and embodiments were famous against personal stench. An answer of natron was utilized to keep bugs from houses . . . Amarna might have been the principal arranger of 'garden city'."

18. Sudan has a larger number of pyramids than some other country on the planet - significantly more than Egypt. There are somewhere around 223 pyramids in the Sudanese urban communities of Al Kurru, Nuri, Gebel Barkal and Meroë. They are by

and large 20 to 30 meters high and steep sided.

19. The Sudanese city of Meroë is wealthy in enduring landmarks. Turning into the capital of the Kushite Realm between 590 BC until Promotion 350, there are 84 pyramids in this city alone, many working with their own small sanctuary. Furthermore, there are vestiges of a shower house imparting affinities to those of the Romans. Its focal element is an enormous pool moved toward by a trip of steps with water prouts enlivened with lion heads.

20. Bling society has a long and intriguing history. Gold was utilized to embellish antiquated Sudanese sanctuaries. That's what one author detailed: "Late unearthings at Meroe and Mussawwarat es-Sufra uncovered sanctuaries with walls and sculptures covered with gold leaf".

21. In around 300 BC, the Sudanese concocted a composing script that had 23 letters of which four were vowels and there was likewise a word divider. Many antiquated texts have endured that were in this content. Some are in plain view in the English Historical center.

22. In focal Nigeria, West Africa's most seasoned civilisation prospered between 1000 BC and 300 BC. Founded in 1928, the old culture was known as the Nok Civilisation, named after the town where the early relics were found. Two current researchers proclaim that "[a]after adjustment, the time of Nok craftsmanship ranges from 1000 BC until 300 BC ". The actual site is a lot more seasoned, returning as soon as 4580 or 4290 BC.

23. West Africans worked in stone by 1100 BC. In the Tichitt-Walata district of Mauritania, archeologists have found "enormous stone workmanship towns" that date back to 1100 BC. The towns consisted of generally round compounds associated with "obvious roads".

24. By 250 BC, the underpinnings of West Africa's most seasoned urban communities were laid out like Old Djenné in Mali.

25. Kumbi Saleh, the capital of Antiquated Ghana, prospered from 300 to 1240 Promotion. Situated in advanced Mauritania, archeological unearthings have uncovered houses, practically tenable today, for need of redesign and a few stories high. They had underground rooms, flights of stairs and associated corridors. Some had nine rooms. A single area of the city is assessed to have housed 30,000 individuals.

26. West Africa had walled towns and urban communities in the pre-pilgrim period. Winwood Reade, an English student of history visited West Africa in the nineteenth 100 years and remarked that: "There are . . . great many enormous walled urban communities looking like those of Europe in the Medieval times, or of antiquated Greece."

27. Ruler Lugard, an English authority, assessed in 1904 that there were 170 walled towns still in existence in the entire Kano area of northern Nigeria.

28. Checks are not exactly as new a creation as we were persuaded to think. In the 10th 100 years, a Bedouin geographer, Ibn Haukal, visited a periphery district of Old Ghana. Writing in 951 Promotion, he recounted a check for 42,000 brilliant dinars

kept in touch with a vendor in the city of
Audoghast by his accomplice in Sijilmassa.

29. Ibn Haukal, writing in 951 Promotion,
illuminates us that the Ruler regarding Ghana
was "the most extravagant lord on the
substance of the earth" whose pre-
prominence was because of the amount of
gold pieces that had been amassed by himself
and by his ancestors.

30. The Nigerian city of Ile-Ife was cleared in
1000 Promotion on the sets of a female ruler
with improvements that started in Old
America. Normally, nobody needs to make
sense of how this occurred roughly 500 years
before the hour of Christopher Columbus!

FACTS ABOUT AFRICA

Africa is the world's second biggest mainland and is home to probably the most lovely nations on the planet with probably the most interesting scenes and untamed life which is the reason it is a top place to get-away. The following are 27 fun realities about Africa and we trust that subsequent to perusing this you will be significantly more captivated about this awesome landmass…

1. THERE ARE 54 Nations IN AFRICA
Africa is the second biggest landmass on the planet and flaunts a bigger number of nations than Asia the biggest mainland on the planet. In sequential request, the nations are as per the following: Algeria, Angola, Benin, Botswana, Burkina Faso, Burundi, Cameroon, Cape Verde, Focal African Republic, Chad, Vote based Republic of the

Congo, Djibouti, Egypt, Central Guinea, Eritrea, Ethiopia, Gabon, Gambia, Ghana, Guinea Bissau, Guinea, Ivory Coast, Kenya, Lesotho, Liberia, Libya, Madagascar, Malawi, Mali, Mauritania, Mauritius, Morocco, Mozambique, Namibia, Niger, Nigeria, Republic of the Congo, Gathering, Rwanda, Senegal, Seychelles, Sierra Leone, Sao Book and Principe, Somalia, South Africa, Sudan, Swaziland, Tanzania, Togo, Tunisia, Uganda, Western Sahara, Zambia and Zimbabwe.

2. AFRICA COVERS 30 MILLION SQUARE Kilometers

Africa is a colossal landmass and it is split into five sub-segments; North Africa, East Africa, Focal Africa, Southern Africa and West Africa. The total of Africa covers right around 10 million square miles which makes up over 20% of the world's territory!

3. THE MOST Broadly Communicated in LANGUAGE IS ARABIC

This might be to some degree an amazing fun reality about Africa. Because of the way that there are 54 nations in Africa, there are various dialects spoken. Nonetheless, the most broadly communicated language here is Arabic (by 170 million individuals), followed by English (by 130 million individuals) then Swahili, French, Bereber, Hausa and Portuguese. There are additionally various dialects that are spoken here which we question that you have even known about…

4. THERE ARE In excess of 2,000 Perceived Dialects

Over a fourth of the various dialects that are all spoken on the planet are spoken in Africa in their relative districts. There are more than 2,000 different perceived dialects spoken in Africa, around 200 of these are spoken in Northern Africa including Focal Sahara and

are known as Afro-Asiatic dialects, 140 are
spoken in Focal and Eastern Africa known as
Nilo-Saharan dialects and more than 1,000
are Niger-Saharan dialects.

5. Lack of education IS Just about as HIGH
AS 40% ACROSS THE Landmass
In spite of the fact that Africa holds various
assets it is a landmass where a considerable
lot of the nations have immense quantities of
their populaces residing in neediness. This
has prompted 40% of grown-ups in Africa
being uneducated. The most awful impacted
regions, with stunning ignorance more than
half are in Ethiopia, Chad, Gambia, Sierra
Leone, Senegal, Niger, Benin and Burkina
Faso.

6. AFRICA IS THE WORLD'S Most blazing
Landmass
As you likely definitely know,
Africa has an extremely warm

environment and being the world's most sizzling continent is really thought of. Around 60% of land is dry and covered by desert, and the Sahara is the world's greatest desert with temperatures frequently besting 100°F (or surpassing 40°C). Be that as it may, while the most smoking recorded temperature on Earth was once in Africa in El Azizia, Libya at 136.4°F (58°C), the mainland likewise has the other limit with the coldest mild in Africa being pretty much as low as −11°F (−23.9 °C) in Ifrane, Morocco. This simply shows the variety of the various nations here in Africa and the distinctions don't end with the environment!

7. AFRICA WAS ONCE Comprised of 10,000 STATES

Before provincial rule, Africa was composed of 10,000 distinct states and independent gatherings, each with their own extremely particular dialects and remarkable traditions. This pre-provincial, disconnected Africa could make sense of why there are such countless dialects spoken and why a considerable lot of the dialects expressed in districts of Africa are not spoken somewhere else

8. ZAMBIA HAD A SPACE PROGRAM During THE 1960S

Despite the fact that it sounds impossible during the 1960s, Zambia was home to a space program, yet it was anything but an extremely effective one. It began in light of the fact that a Zambian resident was determined to beating the Americans and the Russians in being quick to send a man to arrive on the moon. Asides from the space program, there was likewise an award for £7 million that was applied for to send 12 space explorers and a feline to Mars yet this was denied and the space program fizzled. This is most likely our number one fun reality about Africa

9. NIGERIA HAS THE Biggest NUMBER OF TWINS Brought into the world On the planet

Perhaps Africa's biggest nation, Nigeria, has been nicknamed "The Place that is known for Twins" by the BBC on the grounds that it has the most noteworthy pace of twin births on the planet. Numbers show that twin rates of birth in West Africa are multiple times higher here than elsewhere on the planet and the focal point, all things considered, happens in a languid little town in Nigeria considered Igbo-Ora where the last recorded figures uncovered a normal of 50 arrangements of twins in each 1,000 births.

10. North of 5 MILLION Individuals Passed on IN THE Subsequent CONGO WAR

The Subsequent Congo War, which started in August 1998, happened just a single year after the Main Congo War and is the second deadliest overall struggle, resulting just in The Second Great War. The conflict began as a political and military strain among Rwanda and Zaire (presently Equitable Republic of the Congo) and drove later to include seven different nations; in excess of 5 million lives were taken during the Subsequent Congo War. To maintain order and prevent the loss of life from rising, a nonaggression treaty was endorsed in 2002 however a portion of the brutality actually go on today so the DRC is presently viewed as a dangerous to travel.

In any case, don't mistake this for the Republic of Congo which is an extremely protected safari objective (and an extraordinary one at that!)

11. AFRICA Partook IN THE Most brief Conflict At any point Kept IN HISTORY

In addition to the fact that Africa was the host of the second deadliest conflict it was likewise home to the world's most limited war at any point ever. The conflict started in August 1896 and it was among Zanzibar and Extraordinary England. It began in light of the fact that the English didn't acknowledge the progression of Ruler Khalid container Barghash after the past supportive of English Ruler Hamad receptacle Thuwaini. As English powers went after the royal residence grounds, war broke out however the fight just a brief time before Ruler Khalid container Barghash raised the white banner of give up. He later escaped to German East Africa while the English assumed control over issues and selected another Ruler.

12. AROUND 90% OF ALL Jungle fever CASES On the planet ARE IN AFRICA

As you most likely know, Jungle fever is a profoundly destructive illness, especially in Africa. Around 3,000 youngsters pass on from Jungle fever each and every day in Africa and 90% of all Jungle fever cases across the world happen here. We encourage anybody who can give to any of the accompanying causes to assist with saving youngsters needing clinical assistance; Jungle fever No More, Christian Guide, UNICEF or Against Intestinal sickness Establishment. This is a terrible sickness and one that isn't effectively battled when the nation is in such a lot of neediness so any assist that the Western world with canning offer is significant.

13. AFRICA'S SAHARA DESERT IS Greater THAN THE USA

As recently referenced, Africa is the most blazing mainland on earth thus a lot of its property is comprised of desert. The Sahara, being the biggest desert on the planet, is really huge. Its sweeping size is 9.4 million square kilometers - greater than the whole USA! One more fascinating reality about the Sahara is that it is really filling in size as it's been growing in the southern districts at a pace of a portion of a mile each month which likens to six miles each year!

14. THERE ARE Under 9 MILES Isolating AFRICA AND EUROPE

There are numerous distinctions in culture among Africa and Europe, right off the bat since the two of them have such countless various nations with a wide range of societies. In any case, at their nearest point, they are under nine miles separated. At the

Waterway of Gibraltar among Morocco and Spain, there are under nine miles extending the distance and presently the two nations are in discussions about an undersea rail organization to make Africa-Europe travel simpler and more advantageous which would be fabulous for future safari occasions...

15. IT HAS Perhaps OF THE Most seasoned College On the planet

Although numerous grown-ups are unskilled here, Africa is really home to quite possibly the most seasoned college on the planet. Underlying the twelfth 100 years, Timbuktu in Mali had turned into the focal point of all scholarly people and antiquarians have even marked it as the "Paris of Bygone eras". The College of Timbuktu was inherited 982 CE and it is quite possibly the most seasoned known instructive foundation.

16. AFRICA IS HOME TO THE WORLD'S
Greatest FROG SPECIES

It might really not be astounding that the
world's biggest frog species dwells in Africa.
It is named the Goliath Frog and can grow up
to a foot long in size and can weigh up to 8lb
(heavier than the typical human newly
conceived child!). This charming nearly
nothing (or not all that little) animal might be
large however it's innocuous and is tracked
down in Tropical Guinea and Cameroon.

17. IT'S THE Greatest SINGLE Wellspring
OF GOLD All through MINING HISTORY

As we said before, Africa is home to a few
extraordinary assets pursued by the Western
world. Close to half of the gold at any point
mined on Earth has come from Africa, and all
the more explicitly, from Witwatersrand in
South Africa. In spite of the decrease
underway, gold products were valued at $3.8
billion USD back in 2005. South Africa is

likewise renowned for its precious stones, in spite of the fact that Botswana lead the way with regards to creation.

18. AFRICAN ELEPHANTS ARE THE Greatest LAND Vertebrates

African elephants are the biggest living area creatures; they are so huge as a matter of fact that they can weigh north of six tons and depend on seven meters in length in size. They are frequently contrasted with their Asian family members however they have numerous unmistakable contrasts, including the way that they are greater in size! They likewise have a lot bigger ears

CONCLUSION

Assuming you have perused the historical backdrop of Dark American subjection, the social equality, the African-american experience, among other revolting encounters of Individuals of color across the world in previous eras, you would get alternate points of view that continue to hurl numerous unanswered inquiries.

Numerous producers have endeavored to respond to the inquiries by uncovering and causing worldwide to notice Africa's appalling past in unfamiliar terrains with grant wining films like Kunta Kinte. However, there are numerous accounts that should be told.

As of not long ago, very little is had some significant awareness of the Dark English Battle, a terrible encounter of Individuals of color in the Unified Realm before. The battle is one of the narratives that should be told and a movie producer who encountered the fury is presently telling the story to an age that is by all accounts in a rush to fail to remember history.

Adewale Akinnuoye-agbaje, an English Nigerian entertainer, is uncovering the English battle according to his own point of view in the film he named 'Cultivating'. The title alludes to a social practice where Nigerian settlers to England would briefly give their youngsters to white non-permanent families, sending cash for the kid's upkeep while they contemplated to make a superior life for themselves.

The film, which is his directional presentation, depends on Akinnuoye-agbaje's mind boggling story as a pained youth, and as a dark individual from a white skinhead posse in 1980s Essex.

It recounts an account of a youthful Nigerian kid, 'cultivated out' by his folks to a white English family in the desire for a superior future. All things being equal, he turns into the dreaded head of a white skinhead posse. The convincing film sees Akinnuoye-agbaje transform his horrendous early life into a show, yet telling the one of the numerous untold stories.

Akinnuoye-agbaje's folks were among an age of Nigerians to come to England, the pioneer "motherland" to get a college degree, which they could bring back home and use to fabricate a majority rule government in their recently free country, then plagued by nationwide conflict.

The producer was among the numerous Nigerian youngsters taken in by his non-permanent parents and for the most part raised by his new mother, Ingrid (played in the film with rough soul by Kate Beckinsale) while her significant other was away filling in as a truck driver.

Peruse moreover: Whatever happened to Philippines obligation subjugation?

Making sense of the reasoning for making the film, Akinnuoye-agbaje's expressed, "Here in England, we know a great deal about the historical backdrop of Dark American subjection, social equality, and the African American experience. Be that as it may, very little is had some significant awareness of the dark English battle. This is only one of our accounts."

Also, the movie producer followed the beginning of cultivating to a well established propensity in Africa, especially Nigeria where guardians typically send their youngsters from the town to remain with a more distant family member(s) in the municipalities for better open doors, particularly schooling and not really for better childhood.

Yet, in the UK then, at that point, and other unfamiliar grounds, the movie producer noticed that Africans like his folks considered cultivating to be a status thing as "they believed that us should get schooling and figure out how to talk great English".

Nonetheless, the training stayed famous until in 2000 when the regulations became severe following the maltreatment and murder of Victoria Climbié.

In any case, while there were no authority information on the number of African youngsters that were cultivated in the UK for quite a long time, Akinnuoye-agbaje said that most Nigerian English kids experienced basically a couple of years from their introduction to the world families, while the white temporary parents and homes then, at that point, developed.

Most likely because of the untold story it uncovered, the film scooped the Michael Powell Grant for Best English Component Film at the Edinburgh Worldwide Film Celebration (EIFF) this year.

For the EIFF jury individuals, which included; Antonia Campbell-Hughes, David Hayman and Philip John, "The consistent choice of the Michael Powell Jury goes to a significant, strong and upsetting film from Adewale Akinnuoye-Agbaje. This story compels us to go up against a new, awkward reality. Cultivating keeps you put resources into its severe world. Socially adrenalising. Instinctive. Persuasive."

Aslo, a similar j ur y granted the Best Execution in an English Component Film honor to Damson Idris for his job in Cultivating.

Talking on the movie and its accomplishments up until this point, Moses Babatope, overseeing chief, Filmone, Lagos, Nigeria, said that the film is a significant one for the district. "We have such countless stories that should be told. Many, such as Cultivating, have pertinence past Africa and influence the set of experiences and culture of different nations where there is a Nigerian diaspora. We need to guarantee that crowds in West Africa get to watch films that shift the discussion around our effect on the world."

In the mean time, with brilliant names like Genevieve Nnaji, Kate Beckinsale, Gugu Mbatha-crude among others in its gathering, Cultivating is a must-watch due to its chilling tale about confrontational need to overcome the past, prior to embracing an eventual fate of trust.